DINO SAFARI

A LEGO® ADVENTURE IN THE REAL WORLD

by Penelope Arlon
and Tory Gordon-Harris

I've got a bone to pick with you, mister!

SCHOLASTIC

New York   Toronto   London   Auckland
Sydney   Mexico City   New Delhi   Hong Kong

Welcome, LEGO fans!

LEGO® Minifigures show you the world in a unique nonfiction program.

This leveled reader is part of a program of LEGO® nonfiction books, with something for all the family, at every age and stage. LEGO nonfiction books have amazing facts, beautiful real-world photos, and minifigures everywhere, leading the fun and discovery.

To find out about the books in the program, visit www.scholastic.com.

Leveled readers from Scholastic are designed to support your child's efforts to learn how to read at every age and stage.

LEVEL 1 READER

Beginning reader
Preschool–Grade 1
Sight words
Words to sound out
Simple sentences

LEVEL 2 READER

Developing reader
Grades 1–2
New vocabulary
Longer sentences

LEVEL 3 READER

Growing reader
Grades 1–3
Reading for inspiration
and information

Contents

BUILD IT!

Check out the epic building ideas when you see me!

Come on a dinosaur safari with us. Let's see how many dinosaurs we can spot!

I don't like the look of those raptors. I hope that there's nothing bigger out there . . .

Let's find dinos!

It's millions and millions of years ago. There are no houses, no cars, no phones. Our Earth is ruled by the biggest land animals ever—the dinosaurs. Dinosaur explorers need to watch their step.

Let's go! There were 700 kinds of dinosaurs. Let's find as many as we can!

I hear that I might be related to the dinos. I wonder if that's true!

The world is full of huge meat-eaters, and they are all hungry. Run! T. rex wants its breakfast!

BUILD IT!

Build a tall tower for the explorers to climb up and watch the dinosaurs from.

I'll keep you safe and show you what I know. Come on, dino spotters!

This probably isn't the best place for me . . .

5

← **Monolophosaurus**

Meat-eaters

Every day and night in dino world was a food fight. Dinosaurs were either looking for dinner or trying to not be dinner! Meat-eaters had terrible weapons. Huge, razor-sharp teeth crunched through bones like crackers. Claws tore through tough skin like paper. Smaller dinosaurs were just as deadly. They had speed and brains, too.

Some meat-munchers had teeth that curved backward to hold prey.

Utahraptor →

I think I can see the point of those . . . yikes!

ER60082

Giganotosaurus →

← Dilophosaurus

Argh! I'm glad that the dinos will be long gone before people arrive.

BUILD IT!

The explorers need somewhere to shelter. Quick, build a safe, dino-proof hideout!

Spinosaurus ➡

Arrgh! Spinosaurus is coming! Jump in the lake!

Think again! Spinosaurus could swim even faster than it could run!

Take a jaw full of terrifying teeth. Take claws that could slash through a bicycle. Add them to a huge, hungry dinosaur. Say hello to Spinosaurus.

It's the biggest predator of all. Spinosaurus's jaws were as long as your mom or dad!

Compsognathus was built for speed. I'd better run and save my bacon!

◄ Compsognathus

A pack of hungry Velociraptors moves around a Protoceratops. The raptors can bring it down only if they work together. They have large claws on their feet, like daggers. Tiny, sharp teeth are ready to tear into Protoceratops's tough skin.

Protoceratops →

Racing raptors! They've formed a pack, but what are they hunting?

Oh, no! The raptors are after Hot Dog Man! Will they catch up?

Let's hope they don't like mustard.

Waaahh!

But Protoceratops
fights back. It flicks its
thick tail at the raptors.
It bites with its sharp beak.
Who will win?

Hmm . . . Protoceratops lived in a
herd. But even with its friends, I
don't think it could beat the raptors.

Velociraptor had
a larger brain
than other dinos.
This was one
smart dinosaur.

Velociraptor

Velociraptors could
run at 40 miles per
hour (64 kph) in
short bursts.

Plant-eaters

Some dinosaurs ate only plants. You may think that these herbivores were a calm, friendly bunch. THINK AGAIN! They needed epic battle skills to fight off the meat-eaters. Some of them had horns for stabbing. Club-shaped tails could bash and slam. Thick skulls smashed against one another. Thumb spikes gave nasty pokes.

Look at the large, bony bumps. That sharp beak gives me goose bumps, though!

Ankylosaurus

Pachycephalosaurus

← **Torosaurus**

← **Iguanodon**

Skin a quarter inch (6 mm) thick! My suit of armor is no match for that.

13

What's the best way to keep safe from a meat-eater? Have thousands of friends to protect you! Many plant-eaters lived in herds, or groups. There could be 10,000 dinosaurs in just one herd. If a dinosaur had no friends—it had to RUN! Gallimimus was one of the fastest. It could run as fast as a racehorse.

- What's worse than one croc coming for dinner?
- Two crocs coming for dinner!

← **Edmontosaurus**

Okay, let's see how fast this dino can go. They say that it ran at 40 miles per hour (64 kph)!

Gallimimus →

15

Dino fight! It's meat-eater against plant-eater. Allosaurus wants a meal. But it's not going to be easy. Stegosaurus has plates on its back. That's not the place to attack. Allosaurus lunges at the neck. In a flash, Stegosaurus swipes its deadly tail at the meat-eater. But Allosaurus is smart and fast. It will figure out how to get its huge jaws around the plant-eater. Who will win?

Allosaurus's short arms didn't help this meat-eater. It needed big, strong arms that punch like mine . . .

Allosaurus

If Allosaurus won, it had enough food to eat for two weeks.

This is making me hungry. How about enough pizza for two weeks? Yum!

◀ **Stegosaurus**

17

The best way to not be eaten was to be ENORMOUS. Plant-eaters needed to be REALLY enormous, because meat-eaters were supersize, too. How big was Argentinosaurus? This plant-eater was so big that you couldn't get your arms around its leg! Look up at a three-story building. That's how tall this dinosaur was!

Argentinosaurus

At nearly 100 tons, this dino was about as heavy as a jet.

Imagine all the trees that it trampled and mammals that it squished. Let's fly out of here!

BUILD IT!

Think big, and build the most gigantic dinosaur you can imagine.

This vast dino was nearly as long as two tennis courts. That's aces!

Dig up a dino

When people first dug up dinosaur bones, they thought that the bones were from giants or dragons. It's not hard to see why! Some are gigantic. Dinosaur bones were buried over time. After millions of years, some of them turned into rocks, called fossils. Paleontologists dig up fossils and fit them together like jigsaw puzzles. They sometimes get it wrong!

Okay! We've got a big pile of dino bones here. Let's see what you've learned. Put them together!

Hmm . . . just put them together, she says. Where does this one go?

I think you need to bone up on your dinosaurs . . .

BUILD IT!

Build a Jeep to zoom around a fossil site.

These are tools that paleontologists use. Don't break the fossils!

HEARD THIS WORD?

paleontologist: a scientist who studies fossils to learn about plants and animals that lived a long time ago

Snakes alive! Paleontologists found fossils of a snake eating a baby dino. Sssssss-cary!

Ever seen dino poop? It's not just bone fossils that tell us about dinosaurs. There are other clues, too. Footprints in rock show how big a dinosaur was. The distance between footprints can often tell us how fast the dino ran. Dino egg fossils have also been found. Giant poop fossils can tell us what dinos ate!

Stand back! I need to make sure that this dino poop has lost its stink!

This Therizinosaurus egg is the biggest dino egg ever!

There is a bone in this dino's poop, showing its last lunch.

Hmm . . . what can I tell about this dinosaur from the shape of its skull?

Aha! I've discovered a dinosaur nest. Look at all these eggs!

That's no nest. It's a T. rex toilet. And you're hugging a load of old poop!

Dino birds

Sounds crazy, but dino detectives have figured out that birds are related to dinosaurs. Here's the proof. Many dinosaurs were covered in feathers. Some dinosaurs could glide by stretching out feathered arms like wings. Dinosaurs even laid eggs!

Watch out! Low-gliding Microraptor! This dino is one of the smallest ever found. It climbed high into tree and glided through the forest.

Deinonychus →

Nobody knows what color the feathers were. They may have been pink!

Are you seriously telling me that I am related to those dinos?

Absolutely, birdbrain!

A group of Maiasaura moms has found a perfect place to lay eggs. It's a hungry world out there! The dinos nest close to one another for safety. They scoop out shallow holes. Each mother lays 30 to 40 eggs in her nest. Then mom and dad cover

Some dino eggs were the size of chicken eggs. Others were as big as footballs! Ouch!

This nest is egg-cellent . . . Aaarrrrgh!

the nest with rotting plants to keep the eggs warm. When the babies hatch, they are small and weak. The mother has to look after them.

BUILD IT!

How would you keep baby dinos safe? Build a nest with your bricks.

I wonder what noises these dinosaurs made. Did they sing like birds?

A newborn dino hatchling was about the same length as your school ruler.

Good-bye, dinos!

About 65 million years ago, something terrible happened. The big dinosaurs suddenly disappeared. It seems likely that a huge meteorite fell from space. It hit Earth with a massive BANG! It caused earthquakes all over the world. Dust clouds may have blocked sunlight. Many plants died out. There was nothing for the dinosaurs to eat.

HEARD THIS WORD?

meteorite: a piece of rock or metal from space that lands on Earth

Not even I can put this one out. Call 911!

BUILD IT!

It's the end of the dinosaurs! Build a meteorite to crash into your dino world.

Quick! Let's go, before we blow! It looks like the end of our dino safari. But is it really all over?

Don't worry. Remember, birds are related to dinosaurs!

Hmm . . . I'm suddenly feeling a bit spooked by all these birds . . .

Build a LEGO® dino world!

It's a minifigure adventure in dinosaur world! Use your stickers to fill the desert landscape. Look out for the Velociraptors! There may be others hiding nearby . . .

I'm going to get my buns out of here before those dinos see me!

Amazing dino words

detective
A person who solves mysteries.

earthquake
A sudden, violent shaking of the Earth.

fossil
A bone, shell, footprint, or other trace of an animal or plant from millions of years ago, preserved as rock.

glide
To move through the air smoothly and easily.

hatchling
A baby animal that came out of an egg.

herbivore
An animal that eats only plants.

herd
A group of animals that live or travel together.

meteorite
A piece of rock or metal from space that lands on Earth.

paleontologist
A scientist who studies fossils to learn about plants and animals that lived a long time ago.

predator
An animal that hunts and eats other animals.

prey
An animal that is hunted and eaten by another animal.

safari
A trip to see wild animals in their natural surroundings.

skull
The set of bones in the head that protects the brain.

Dino names

Allosaurus
AL-uh-SOR-uhs

Ankylosaurus
ANG-kuh-luh-SOR-uhs

Argentinosaurus
AHR-juhn-TEE-nuh-SOR-uhs

Compsognathus
kahmp-SAHG-nuh-thuhs

Deinonychus
dye-nah-NIK-uhs

Dilophosaurus
dye-LOH-fuh-SOR-uhs

Edmontosaurus
ed-MAHN-tuh-SOR-uhs

Gallimimus
gal-uh-MYE-muhs

Giganotosaurus
JEE-gan-oh-tuh-SOR-uhs

Iguanodon
ig-WAH-nuh-dahn

Maiasaura
MYE-uh-SOR-uh

Microraptor
MYE-kroh-RAP-tur

Monolophosaurus
MAHN-uh-loh-fuh-SOR-uhs

Pachycephalosaurus
pak-ee-SEF-uh-luh-SOR-uhs

Protoceratops
proh-toh-SER-uh-tahps

Spinosaurus
SPYE-noh-SOR-uhs

Stegosaurus
STEG-uh-SOR-uhs

Therizinosaurus
THER-uh-ZEE-nuh-SOR-uhs

Torosaurus
TOR-oh-SOR-uhs

T. rex
TEE reks

Utahraptor
YOO-tah-RAP-tur

Velociraptor
vuh-LAH-suh-RAP-tur

Index

Credits

For the LEGO Group: Randi Kirsten Sørensen Assistant Manager; Peter Moorby Licensing Coordinator; Heidi K. Jensen Licensing Manager; Paul Hansford Creative Publishing Manager; Martin Leighton Lindhardt Publishing Graphic Designer

Photographs ©: cover dinosaurs: Jon Hughes; cover background: Maksym Gorpenyuk/Dreamstime; back cover background: Maksym Gorpenyuk/Dreamstime; back cover dinosaur: Valentyna Chukhlyebova/Shutterstock, Inc.; 1 background: Kurt Drubbel/iStockphoto; 1 dinosaur: Jon Hughes; 2-3 sky background: tupungato/iStockphoto; 2-3 ferns: Papa Bravo/Shutterstock, Inc.; 2-3 dinosaurs: Jon Hughes; 4-5 dinosaurs: Jon Hughes; 6-7 bones: VvoeVale/iStockphoto; 6-7 dinosaurs: Jon Hughes; 8-9 dinosaurs: Jon Hughes; 10-11 dinosaurs: Jon Hughes; 12 center fern: dabjola/iStockphoto; 12-13 ferns: Elenathewise/iStockphoto; 12-13 ferns: shulz/iStockphoto; 12-13 dinosaurs: Jon Hughes; 14 waterfall: yulkapopkova/iStockphoto; 14-15 dinosaurs: Jon Hughes; 15 ferns: J.Y. Loke/Shutterstock, Inc.; 15 rock: AndreaAstes/iStockphoto; 16-17 dinosaurs: Jon Hughes; 18-19 sky background: Noppol Mahawanjam/iStockphoto; 18-19 dinosaurs: Jon Hughes; 19 ferns: Elenathewise/iStockphoto; 19 ferns: shulz/iStockphoto; 20-21 background: John Elk III/Alamy Images; 21 tools: Ted Kinsman/Science Source; 22 top left: Louie Psihoyos/Corbis Images; 22 bottom right: gfrandsen/iStockphoto; 22 magnifying glass: mizar_21984/Fotolia; 22-23 bottom background: Maxfocus/iStockphoto; 23 top: MarquesPhotography/iStockphoto; 24 bottom left rock: AndreaAstes/iStockphoto; 24 bottom left ferns: kcrep/iStockphoto; 24 top ferns: Dole08/iStockphoto; 24-25 dinosaurs: Jon Hughes; 24-25 top background rocks: Romariolen/iStockphoto; 26 center fern: shulz/iStockphoto; 26-27 background: changwong/iStockphoto; 26-27 dinosaurs: Jon Hughes; 26-27 egg nests: Roberto Nistri/Alamy Images; 28-29 dinosaurs: Jon Hughes; 30 dinosaur: Jon Hughes; 30-31 background: Kurt Drubbel/iStockphoto.

All LEGO® illustrations and stickers by Paul Lee.

And thanks to me, everyone survived this hair-raising, bone-crunching safari. Whew!

ISBN 978-0-545-94766-4

10 9 8 7   17 18 19 20

Printed in the U.S.A.   40
First edition, July 2016

ISBN: S-TK5-94766-9   PO# 579344